Complex Conditions

Hope Cherkassky

India | USA | UK

Presentation by *BookLeaf Publishing*

Web: www.bookleafpub.com

E-mail: info@bookleafpub.com

ISBN: 9789358319736

First edition 2023

Sally

Sally
Hypermobile
Stretching, bending, Popping
Body   is   disintegrating
O v e   r   s   t   r e t c h e d

H.E.D.S.

Hypermobile
Everything falling out of place
Dehydration constantly
Stretching past your limits

The Moment Between Us

Able-bodied
strong and active
working, driving, building
genetics, sickness ,accident, age
forcing, accommodating, resting
weak and forgotten
Disabled

Ehlers Danlos Syndrome

Genetic syndrome
Affecting my whole being
Comorbidities

Flare

Like fire ants biting
Their acid searing my joints
My pains are valid
Not made up for attention
They're simply invisible

Tachycardia

6

Feel my heart beating
Like a clock out of rhythm
Don't try to stand up
Allergic to gravity
Time for compression and salt

Compensating

All of my life I have been compensating
For a body that was constantly breaking
Redefining who I am, and what I can do
Learning when it's not okay to push through
Finding joy in the smaller things
Allowing myself to feel my feelings
Learning dreams don't always come true
In the ways I might expect them to
Learning it's not conducive
To always be productive
Knowing which muscles to tighten
Seeing where my load should lighten
Allowing my self to rest when needed
And making sure my body is heeded
For all of my life I will be compensating
For a body that is still always breaking

Airplane

Sometimes I feel like I should be able to fly
then suddenly I slam into the pavement
totally aghast, I wonder
As if I had never tried before
Craaaack
Pain in every crevice of my being
tears stinging my eyes
I should have known I couldn't fly
I have no wings.
This isn't an inspirational story of overcoming
but of learning to thrive within these limitations
A mixture of capitalism and fear causes
Society to furrow their brow and say:

"You can do anything you will" and "you must
not be wishing hard enough"

I've wanted nothing more than to fly since I
could say the word
Yet, anyone will laugh and tell you it's
rediculous to fly without wings,
and to just use an airplane

Vertigo

The room is spinning, or is it my head ?
This familiar feeling feels me with dread
Like a rubberband with no give
difficulty being active
I know this feeling will pass with rest
But it still feels like I have a stampede in my
chest

Release

Immeasurable tension building
Muscles threatening to rip
 like shredding chicken
joints slipping out of their sockets
Then I apply a gentle pressure
A controlled pain , heat, and release
The pain melts away
The stiffness replaced with soft warmth
I remember what this body used to feel like
I can breath again
For now.

Internalized

I love my wheelchair
It helps me when
I am too sick to stand
 conserve energy
And do things I
normally can't do
And yet
I hate that my wheelchair
Comes with stares
And people asking
"what happened to you"
 thinking I am too lazy
Am I really too lazy?

And then I stop
Take a breath
people may stare
And use careless words
But then I realize
the sharpest words
Are actually me.

Warrior

After years of living with this condition
I realize my body is not the enemy
I am not at war with myself anymore
We have signed a peace treaty
My body is not a prison
My life is worth living
Fighting an imaginary war gets tiring
And I need to conserve my energy
And realize I am not a warrior
We are both just trying to stay alive

When I got sick

When I got sick I found out really fast
Who my friends were and who they weren't.
People I thought would stay forever were
suddenly making excuses to stay away

When I got sick I found out really fast
Who my family was and who they weren't
Losing family members who promised
They would always be there for me

When I got sick I learned who I am
How strong and resilliant I can be
How to ask for help when needed
And how to pick my chosen family

Complex

Complex Conditions
Always leave doctors guessing
It's not in your head

Ode to Salt

Your white crystals shake

making food delicious

Sprinkling onto everything

From savory to sweet.

Just a pinch to add depth

And to form icecream

You balance with water

In order to support life

In my blood flowing

You keep me upright

and compliment Fries

So perfectly

A lot

I have a deep fear of losing you
That this condition will rip us in two.
One day you will realize it's just too much
And resent me for the feelings you clutch
Only seeing yourself as my caregiver
and viewing me as just another taker

then I remember, that I am in fact a lot
a lot of love, kindness and care,
 Loving wife, and copilot
future mother extraordinaire
 I am no less worthy of love
 because I am sick
 truly, I am one badass chick.

But you know all of this.
I am just reminding myself

Good Vibes

My disability is part of me and it cannot be
separated
Prayers and good vibes will only leave you
frustrated
I don't want your herbs, yoga , tinctures or detox
diet
I promise you that if it worked , I'd have already
tried it.
I am not malingering or seeking attention
I don't need your help or your condescension
Please leave me alone and go on your way
I have a ton of medical appointments today

Ambulatory

Somedays use a cane,
Need my wheelchair on others,
All days are valid

Accessibility Parking

Park closer next time
I am getting too fatigued
I will use my chair

Dysautonomia

Dizziness hits like a sudden crash
Yesterday I felt okay, but now I'm
Slowly slipping out of consciousness
Audio and vision getting fuzzy
Unable to move, talk or think
Tachycardia amd palpitations
Orthostatic intolerance, My heart is
Not pumping blood to my brain
Only pooling in my extremities
My feet are turning violet
I wake up fatigued and blurry
All I did to cause this was stand

MCAS

21

Mediators spontaneously released
Causing systemic symptoms all over
Allergic reactions and anaphylaxis
Someone please get my epi-pen